Mission:Explore

The Geography Collective

First published in Great Britain in 2010

by Can of Worms Kids Press
7 Peacock Yard
Iliffe Street
London
SE17 3LH

www.canofwormsenterprises.co.uk
www.missionexplore.co.uk

Copyright © Can of Worms Enterprises 2010
Text copyright © The Geography Collective
Illustrations copyright © Tom Morgan-Jones
Design by Emily Atkins
Cover by Helen Steer

All rights reserved. No part of this publication
may be reproduced, stored in a retrieval system or
transmitted in any form or by any means without
the prior written permission of the publisher nor
be otherwise circulated in any form of binding or
cover other than that in which it is published and
without a similar condition being imposed on the
subsequent purchaser.

A catalogue record for this book is available from
the British Library.

ISBN: 978-1-904872-33-7

DISCLAIMER: Every care has been taken in providing
safety tips for Mission Explorers, but neither the
authors nor the publishers can take responsibility
for any injuries or harmful effects resulting from
their actions - don't say we haven't warned you!

Printed in the UK by J F Print Ltd., Sparkford, Somerset.

Mission:Explore

The Geography Collective

Illustrations by Tom Morgan-Jones

Published by The Can of Worms Kids Press

Dear Explorer,

We are delighted that you have made it this far. As you will see, this is no ordinary book. Do not go any further if you are afraid of going on adventures or trying new things. There is a severe risk that you will never see the world in the same way again.

Over the following pages you will discover over 100 missions, 102 to be exact. Your challenge is to complete and record each of them as best you can. By the time you have completed your unique copy of this book you will be a hardened explorer, extreme missioner and have a new-found expertise in guerrilla geography.

Before you accept any missions in this book, complete our Explorer Basic Training and make sure you have permission for your plans and that they are reasonably safe.

It's time to explore,

The Geography Collective

CONTENTS

- [ ] ME0025 Capture a memory
- [ ] ME0026 Swatch nature
- [ ] ME0027 Establish a new country
- [ ] ME0028 R.I.P.
- [ ] ME0029 Go photo orienteering
- [ ] ME0030 Go hunting for mini-beasts
- [ ] ME0031 Make your local area more friendly
- [ ] ME0032 Go somewhere new
- [ ] ME0033 Make this page smell of summer
- [ ] ME0034 Name the friendliest restaurant in town
- [ ] ME0035 Discover common people
- [ ] ME0036 Leave evidence that we walked on our hands
- [ ] ME0037 Sell the smell of your town
- [ ] ME0038 Make up a word
- [ ] ME0039 Celebrate a national holiday in style
- [ ] ME0040 Wear ear plugs for a day
- [ ] ME0041 Call a local phone box
- [ ] ME0042 Become a pet detective
- [ ] ME0043 Find the tallest tree
- [ ] ME0044 Play dare with a chair
- [ ] ME0045 Travel with your mind
- [ ] ME0046 Become a hero
- [ ] ME0047 Rubbish map
- [ ] ME0048 Discover a new life form
- [ ] ME0049 Converse with a cow
- [ ] ME0050 Use less water
- [ ] ME0051 Make an Earth sandwich
- [ ] ME0052 Sketch the view
- [ ] ME0053 Switch sides
- [ ] ME0054 Create a political walk
- [ ] ME0055 Find the highest...
- [ ] ME0056 Raise money

- [ ] ME0057 Whisper like a spy
- [ ] ME0058 Go for a back-to-front walk
- [ ] ME0059 Set up a teddy blog
- [ ] ME0060 Write a strange(r) play
- [ ] ME0061 Picture talk
- [ ] ME0062 Be random
- [ ] ME0063 Block your senses
- [ ] ME0064 Navigate like a bat
- [ ] ME0065 Defy gravity
- [ ] ME0066 Find a non-native animal
- [ ] ME0067 Discover the best garden
- [ ] ME0068 Escape
- [ ] ME0069 Talk international
- [ ] ME0070 Dress as a ...., ...
- [ ] ME0071 Picture a year
- [ ] ME0072 Make a ghost town
- [ ] ME0073 Look north
- [ ] ME0074 Memorise a place
- [ ] ME0075 Make your area better
- [ ] ME0076 Squeeze in
- [ ] ME0077 Play hide in shop
- [ ] ME0078 Visit a place of worship
- [ ] ME0079 See a place differently
- [ ] ME0080 Go on a random adventure
- [ ] ME0081 Look up
- [ ] ME0082 Place a soundtrack
- [ ] ME0083 Broadcast to the world
- [ ] ME0084 Conduct an economic experiment
- [ ] ME0085 Use your flower power
- [ ] ME0086 Play pavement games
- [ ] ME0087 Go on the wetter run
- [ ] ME0088 Record a place

WARNING!

This book can be dangerous.
Do not:

1. attempt to eat it

2. throw it at people

3. do anything that may harm people,
wildlife or the environment.

WARNING!

Attempting to complete the missions
in this book will result in exciting
explorations and brushes with danger.
The authors take no responsibility for
your safety when attempting missions -
that's your job.

Before attempting any mission in this book, if there is a risk of something or someone getting damaged try and remove the danger. Only attempt the mission if you can do it reasonably safely.

For example, roads kill lots more people than pigeons. Reduce the risk of a car damaging you by using a zebra crossing.

Basic
Training

Explorer basic training

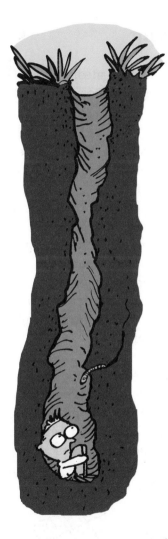

Even the best explorers get into trouble sometimes. To make sure that they can get help if they're attacked by a gammy pigeon or get stuck down a hole they follow this advice, and you should do the same. That way you can still be exploring for many years to come. You'll also avoid getting into unnecessary trouble.

Before starting

☐ Get permission to do the mission and make sure the weather is not going to turn dangerous.

☐ Make sure you let someone know where you are going and what time you'll be back.

☐ Always pack some basic kit: a watch, a fully-charged phone or some change for a phone box and basic survival kit (including any medication you take, some plasters, a snack and drink). Pack a map and compass too for navigating and marking discoveries.

☐ Get into a team whenever doing the more challenging missions. Three is a magic number. If one of you gets hurt, one person can stay with them while the other goes for help. Agree a call (hoooo!) sign and a place where you can meet if you get split up.

☐ Hatch a plan in case it all goes wrong. Where could you go to get help? Who would you call?

Basic training: be mission safe

Emergency contacts

Make sure you know who to contact in an emergency. Write their numbers here:

Emergency contact 1:

Emergency contact 2:

Emergency contact 3:

Emergency Services
(Ambulance, Fire, Police):

The number 112 can be used for emergencies in most countries.

Emergencies

If the mission goes pear-shaped follow
these three steps:

1. Don't panic!

2. Call your emergency contact, tell them
what has happened and where you are.

3. Stay where you are and wait for them
to arrive.

If you need to do some first aid take a
look at the back of this book for some
tips and tricks on what to do.

Use this space to write down what has happened and where here.

You and your team

All the best explorers have rules that they never break. Here are some to help you keep your head on:

☐ Follow what warning signs say and follow any rules that you know of.

☐ Always let an adult know where you're going and what time you'll get back.

☐ Make sure that you look after your friends and don't be persuaded to take silly risks.

☐ If you get injured make sure you tell someone who knows what to do.

☐ Never use kit that you need training for e.g. climbing ropes; they won't keep you safe if you don't know how to use them.

☐ Never go into a stranger's car or house.

☐ Always take the right supplies: juice, fruit, snacks, chocolate and most importantly... water!

☐ Don't stick anything in your mouth if you don't know what it is. You don't want to be poisoned and start puking up over everything.

People, wildlife and places

☐ Protect and care for all people
animals, plants and places you visit.

☐ Whenever possible, leave no trace that
you have even been to a place or
completed the mission. Leave anything,
from gates and hedges to ruins and
parrots, as you find them. Dispose of
rubbish appropriately or take it home
with you.

☐ If you're taking a dog, cat, pigeon or
other animal with you make sure it's
under your control.

☐ Say hello to the people you meet.
They'll like that and you'll like it
when they say hello back.

☐ Be honest and take responsibility if
things go wrong. You'll get far more
respect.

Geography

Geography is about curiosity, exploration and discovery. It gives you the power to see places in new ways, even imaginary ones. Geography also helps you to understand and make sense of the world.

To be a successful geographer you should:

- think of your own questions
- search for your own answers
- talk, watch and listen to people, animals, plants and places
- think about who you are and the effects of your actions

Geographers use many different 'ings' to research, share and act on discoveries. Practice your ings to improve your ability to do missions including: observing, reading, drawing, rubbing, digging, mapping, climbing, ducking, conversing, comparing, photographing, testing, seeking, peeking, clucking, barking, graphing, and searching.

Guerrilla Geography

You can do the missions in this book just for fun. You can also do them to become a Guerrilla (not gorilla) Geographer.

As a Guerrilla Geographer you will ask questions about places and encourage other people to ask questions too. Guerrilla Geographers believe in the importance of justice and things being fair and friendly for people, wildlife and places.

Some of the missions you do will challenge people to think about things that are important to you. Other missions will get you or other people thinking geographically at what may seem unusual or unexpected times. Of course, it's also about having loads of fun having adventures and discovering new things.

Advanced training

If you fancy getting your missions to the next level join a club! There are loads out there that can offer you more advanced training. They have the right professionals with the best kit. If you join, you'll be tooled up for even bigger explorations in no time. Turn to page 194 for a list of websites to find out more.

Completing a mission

This book is for drawing, scrawling, rubbing, scenting, scribbling, illustrating, printing, writing, scraping, dribbling and sticking in.

Make sure you remember pencils and other tools to record your efforts and findings.

Reporting a mission

The best way to report on a mission
is by letting your friends and family
know about what you found out on your
explorations. You can also take your
success global by setting up a blog or
if you are old enough, using Twitter.

You can publicly celebrate your efforts
online with Twitter by using the special
MISSION:EXPLORE codes on each page. The
first mission in this book is ME0001, so
when you've completed it, just include
this code in your tweet. Of course, you
can read other people's recent reports
by searching for mission codes on the
site.

You can also report your missions to us
at The Geography Collective. We will be
ecstatic to read your reports and will
publish some on our website.

www.missionexplore.co.uk

The Missions

Follow a friend

Cut eyeholes in a newspaper and then secretly follow some friends.

How long can you go without being seen?

Put OAPs in the hood

Ask some old people you know to hang out in hoodies on a street corner.

How do people react to them?

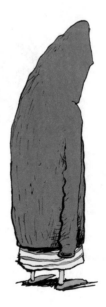

Forget the Internet

Post paper blog entries on your street.

WARNING!

It is illegal to put up posters without permission. If you can't get permission to use your street, ask your local Mayor for a space on your local community notice board.

Turn to stone

Walk down your high street and turn to stone every time someone with a beard looks at you. Record how many times you freeze here.

Make a giant sign

Tip:
Creating big signs can be tricky.
Writing it over a grid first can help
you to make the sign in smaller parts
and make the sign look good.

Use the grid to design and make a word,
sentence or image that people can read/
see when flying past or overlooking it.

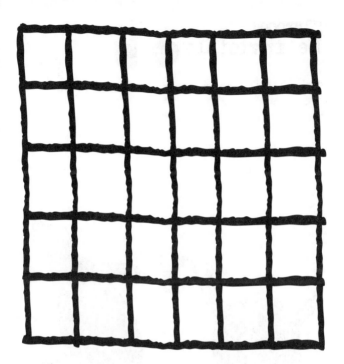

Now go and make it on a beach, field or playground!

 WARNING!

Make sure your sign will not worry or upset anyone. Go to bit.ly/signaldistress to learn about distress signals so you only make one if you mean to!

Be invisible ●.●

Travel 100 metres without being seen.

Record how far you manage to go in each of these environments.

Deciduous woodland: ....

Evergreen forest: ....

Sand dunes: ....

Town centre: ....

Supermarket: ....

Corridors: ....

WARNING!

This Mission:Explorer is wearing a carefully designed bin costume. Don't go inside bins, they're dirty and you may end up puking everywhere or worse!

Be on TV

Put on a performance for a CCTV
controller. You could improvise a short
play, show off a dance routine or hold a
full blown talent show.

Mark out your stage and where the best CCTV cameras are for your performance.

Spend a day without turning anything on

(and you're not allowed to ask anyone to do it for you!)

Walk on the wild side

There are many different paths - choose
one you have never taken before.

Stick something you find here.

Become an extreme stair climber

Climb to the top of the world's highest places without leaving home.

1. Find a staircase. How high is one step?

2. Divide the height of the mountain by the height of one of your steps.

3. Climb that many steps to get to the top! Tick each place off as you conquer it!

☐ Mt Everest 8,848m / 29,029ft

☐ Mt McKinley 6,194m / 20,320ft

☐ Mt Kilimanjaro 5,895m / 19,341ft

☐ Ben Nevis 1,344m / 4,409ft

Search for the heights of other
mountains or buildings to see what else
you can climb.

Map (un)friendly places

Where is (un)friendly in your local area? Create a map across the page to show where the friendliest places are.

49

Investigate the murder of an animal

Next time you find a dead animal, draw a white line around its body and find out who killed it, how, when, where, and why. Fill in the incident report opposite.

WARNING!

It's never a good idea to touch a dead animal, especially if its oozing stuff! You may end up throwing up everywhere or worse. Never do this mission on roads or runways or you could be next....

INCIDENT REPORT

Animal type:

Location of death:

Time of death:

Cause of death:

Significant evidence:

Motivation for the killing:

Suspects:

☐ ME0013
Find a red stone

Paint a stone red. Leave it somewhere
and then come back at a later date to
see if you can find it again.

Draw a map of the local area where you leave the stone. Mark and date where the stone is each time you come back.

Track kangaroos

Foxes, deer, sheep and wheelie bins can all leave trails. Find one, and track down its owner.

Try leaving a false trail for someone by redesigning the bottom of your shoes. Can you persuade someone that there is a kangaroo on the loose?

Does rain fall evenly?

Put identical containers outside in different places... does one fill more than the others?

Let a dog take you for a walk

You are now a dog (you can even go on all fours if you like).

Let a dog take you for a walk and then think about how you sensed the world differently.

What did you...

See?

Smell?

Hear?

Touch?

WARNING!

You may be very tempted, but don't sniff dogs' bums or pooh. You might slip!

☐ ME0016a
Draw the dog that took you for a walk

Follow command signs

Explore your local area looking for signs and words that command you to do things. If you find one, do what it says.

What have the signs made you do? List your actions here:

What can you encourage people to do?
Design and create your own command(o)
sign.

Keep a tally below showing how many
people do what they are told. ·

Hold a dry swimming race

Use some skateboards to hold a dry
swimming championship.

The winner gets:

....

WARNING!

Read the landscape of where you are
going to have your race. Avoid steep
hills, brick walls, and other dangerous
features.

Front crawl

1st:

2nd:

Butterfly

1st:

2nd:

Backstroke

1st:

2nd:

Breaststroke

1st:

2nd:

Collect A-Z

Collect 26 photos of the
letters A-Z in different
places. Cut out and stick
your A-Z over these pages.

Stick your photos here.

Stick your photos here.

65

Go alphabet shopping

Go alphabet shopping. Start at one end
of your local high street and find the
letter 'A' in a shop name and then 'B'
until you find 'Z'. Write the names of the
shops below.

A ....

B ....

C ....

D ....

E ....

F ....

G ....

H ....

I ....

J ....

K ....

L ....

M ....

N ....

O ....

P ....

Q ....

R ....

S ....

T ....

U ....

V ....

W ....

X ....

Y ....

Z ....

Blindfold yourself

Get a friend to help you and explore
just by smell. What can you find?

Plug in and turn off

Put on some headphones and pretend
to be listening to music. Try nodding
your head and bouncing a knee. Listen
carefully to what people are saying
around you.

Fill in the radar map below to record
what you hear.

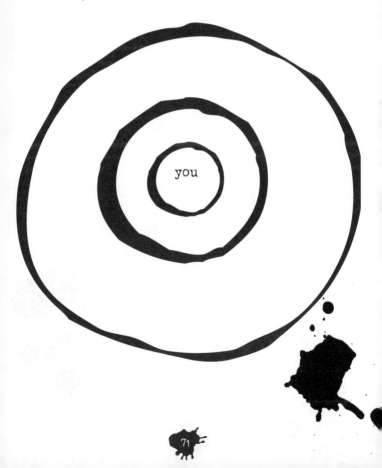

you

Go the mint stint

How far can you travel while sucking
the same mint?

Attempt 1
Create map here

Attempt 2
Create map here

Attempt 3
Create map here

□ ME0024
Say hello to your neighbour

Get to know your neighbour.

Discover:

- where they are from.

- what they like to do.

- if they would like to have a street party.

Pass on this mission to your neighbour and then ask them to pass it on again and then again and again until everyone on your street knows each other.
Is there going to be a street party?

Yes / No

□ ME0025
Capture a memory

Go for a walk, bring back your
favourite memory and then recreate it.

Swatch nature

Pick up a colour swatch from a local
paint shop.

What can you find in nature that
matches any of the colours?

Stick your swatch
here and label it with
what you find.

☐ ME0027

Establish a new country

Get a group of people together and establish your own country by writing to the United Nations. Make sure that you include:

Country name: ....

Claimed land: ....

Leader's name: ....

Leader's position: ....

Political system: ....

Job titles: ....

....

....

....

Design your flag here:

Other important jobs:

Design a stamp

Write a national anthem

Choose a national plant and animal

Create some laws

☐ ME0028
R.I.P.

Find the oldest person buried in your local graveyard. Leave a flower on their grave.

Do a rubbing of part of their
gravestone here:

Go photo orienteering

Take photographs of local places and
then print them off. Can your friends
find the places where the photographs
were taken?

Go hunting for mini-beasts

How many insects and animals can you find in your garden, bedroom, local pond?

Draw the most beastly one here:

WARNING!

Take care around water - you really don't want to end up in it, especially if it's fast, deep, or full of dangerous animals!

Make your local area more friendly

How friendly is your local area? Create and carry out a survey to find out and then write to your local politician about your findings. What can they do to improve things for kids?

Tip: If you write to your local politician they are highly likely to reply.

Stick reply here.

Go somewhere new

Go somewhere you've never been, just to
see what's there.

Record your findings here:

□ME0033

Make this page smell of summer

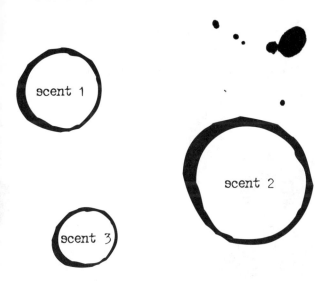

scent 1

scent 2

scent 3

Name the friendliest restaurant in town

Visit some local restaurants. Which is the friendliest to young people? Draft a review below and then send it to your local newspaper.

Discover common people

Sit with someone
your own age
who you don't
know. Talk to
them until you
find a person in
common.

Draw how you are connected below.

Leave evidence that we homo sapiens walked on our hands

Petrified footprints (fossils of footprints) have been found that are thousands of years old. Scientists can use the footprints to discover things about the people who left them. Confuse future scientists by making it look like people alive now walked around on our hands. To pull off this trick just follow these instructions:

1. On a hot and sunny day pour a bucket of water over some muddy ground.

2. Do a handstand into the mud, making sure you leave some great handprints. If you can, walk on them.

3. Leave to harden and then fill them with sand.

Leave for a further 5,000 years for someone to find – and think that humans used to walk around on their hands.

Tip: To increase your chances of this mission working do some research into how Trace fossils are made.

Sell the smell of your town

Bottle the smell of different towns.

Which can you sell for the highest price on the Internet?

Town .... sold for ....

Town .... sold for ....

Town .... sold for ....

☐ME0038
Make up a word

Make up a word.

Word:

Definition:

Synonyms:
(words that mean the same thing)

Start saying it around the place. Where does it catch on? Who do you hear using it?

Celebrate a national holiday in style

Wear the BIGGEST POSSIBLE symbol of your national holiday... say hello to everyone else who's sporting a symbol that day too!

Design your outfit here:

Wear ear plugs for a day

Try cutting out sound from your day.
Put some plugs (ones made to go into
your ears) in and go about your day.

What's easier?

What's harder?

What's the same?

☐ ME0041
Call a local phone box

Find the phone numbers for some local
phone boxes.

Box

Location: .... Number: ....

Location: .... Number: ....

Location: .... Number: ....

Call them and carry out a random survey
to find out what their favourite ....
.... is.

Record the answers below.

Become a pet detective

Study cats. How do they get from one
place to another? How fast can they
travel? Make a map revealing local cat
routes including symbols for danger
spots, hiding places, prey and predators.

Can you return a lost cat to its owners?

WARNING!

Do not follow cats along fence tops.

Now do the same for dogs.....

Find the tallest tree

Use the Internet to discover the best
way to calculate the height of a tree.
Have a competition with some friends to
see who can find the tallest tree.

Species: ....

Height: ....

Width: ....

Get this page to look and smell a little
like the tallest tree you find. Rub this
page gently against the tree's bark.

☐ME0044
Play dare with a chair

Randomly put a chair in a park. Hide.

Who dares to sit on it first?

Draw a picture of them below.

Return the chair!

Travel with your mind

Find a plane in the sky. Shut your eyes and imagine where it is going.

Go there in your mind. What's it like there? What happens? Write a postcard to a friend.

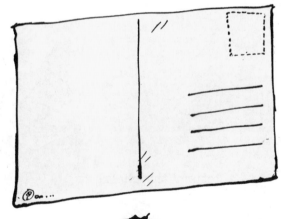

☐ ME0046
Become a hero

Save a falling leaf from hitting the
ground.

Create a rubbing of
your leaf here.

```
┌ ─ ─ ─ ─ ─ ─ ┐
|             |
|             |
|             |
|             |
|             |
|             |
|             |
|             |
|             |
└ ─ ─ ─ ─ ─ ─ ┘
```

□ ME0047
Rubbish map

Look at litter from your local area
and see where it has come from. Draw a
map to show which countries the rubbish
has come from. Can you calculate how
many miles it has travelled before being
dumped?

WARNING!

Wear gloves or
use a grabber and
don't go picking up
filthy sharp stuff.

Draw map here:

Discover a new life form

Ask for permission to let a square metre
of your garden or a local green space
overgrow. Count the different plants and
animals that appear over time.

Week	No. of plants	No. of animals

Tip:
This is best done starting in spring and into the summer.

Converse with a cow

WARNING!

They are usually friendly, but around
two people are trampled to death each
year by cows in Britain. That's not many,
but unless you know the cow it may be
best to stay on the opposite side of the
fence.

Use less water

Watch your house's water meter. Try to get through the next day by using less water than the previous one.

How many days can you do this for?

WARNING!

Do not go thirsty or lose friends for being stinky when attempting this mission.

Make an Earth sandwich

Place a slice of bread on the surface
of our planet at exactly the same
time as someone on the opposite side
of the Earth.

Stick a photograph of your half of
the sandwich here.

Find out more and map your effort
by uploading your photographs to
Ze Frank's sandwich website:
www.zefrank.com/sandwich

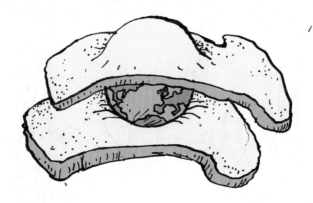

WARNING!

Attempting to eat this sandwich will
have disastrous consequences!

Sketch the view

...from a window.

Switch sides

On your daily journey use only one
side of the road, and the next day use
the opposite. How was the experience
different?

☐ ME0054
Create a political walk

Design a walk to show your local
community what you think of a place.
Get your walk published in your local
paper.

Stick a route map here.

Find the highest...

...and lowest points in
your local village,
town and/or city. Go
there.

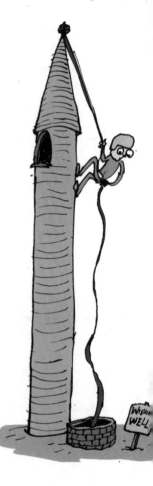

WARNING!

The person in the
cartoon is a highly
trained cartoon adult.
You are not! Trying
to abseil from a
tower into a well is a
highly unusual thing
to do. If you want to
do this, join a club
and get trained up!

Stick something from each place here.

Raise money

How much money can you make for a good
cause by selling things that you no
longer need? List what you sell and how
much for: What can the charity do with
the money you have raised?

WARNING!

Only go into an attic with permission
from the person who owns the ladder.

Whisper like a spy

Sit next to a friend that you have
not spoken to for a while. Whisper the
secret code, 'the birds fly tonight', look
furtive and walk off.

Go for a back-to-front walk

Put your clothes on back to front and go for a walk. What happens?

Set up a teddy blog

Create a blog about a walkabout teddy.
Leave the teddy on public transport
with a note. Ask who finds it to take it
home for a week and to comment on your
blog to say where the teddy is living.
Ask the person to then let the teddy go
walkabout again after a week with the
same rules. Where does the teddy travel?

WARNING!

For tips on keeping safe on the web
visit www.thinkuknow.co.uk

Write a strange(r) play

Go to a charity shop and buy some
random clothes that used to belong to
other people. Use the space below to
describe their characters, who they were
and what they were like.

Draft and perform a
short play about the
strangers who used
to wear the clothes.

Picture talk

Use this space to communicate only
through pictures for one day.

☐ ME0062
Be random

Leave a random object
in a random place.

Record random people's
reactions to your
randomly placed
random object by
completing the random
faces randomly below.

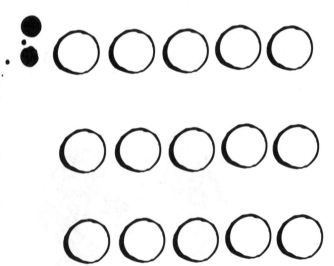

Block your senses

Explore using one sense at a time.
What do you notice and not notice?

(Explore using sonar)

Navigate like a bat

ME0064

Defy gravity

Stay entirely in the air for as long
as possible. Jump! What number can you
count to before you touch back down to
Earth?

WARNING!

Clearly, jumping off high places could
seriously hurt you. You're not a bird,
you can't fly. Don't jump from any
surfaces (that are too high).

Find a non-native animal

...that is living wild in your neighbourhood. Create a food web to show how your exotic creature fits into your local ecosystem.

WARNING!

Don't pick up potentially dangerous animals like crocodiles; you could lose a big chunk of your body.

Discover the best garden

Give marks out of
10 to all the front
gardens on a street.

Mark them for how
they look;

then for how they smell;

then for how good they are for wildlife;

then variety of shapes/colours/plants.

Get a friend to do the same and compare
scores.

Go back 2 months later and repeat.

Escape

Where is your best
escape route? Use
this space to plan
an escape.

Talk international

Every time someone calls your house ask
them where they are calling from. Draw
a line on a map from where they are to
where you are. If they call again make
the line thicker. Where in the world are
you most connected to?

Dress as a ...., ...

Walk down your local high street dressed as different things. Which draws the...

Best look:

Worst look:

Funniest look:

Saddest look:

Worst sound:

Funniest sound:

Saddest sound:

Picture a year

Take a photo every day for a year.
Create a photobook for your friends and
family to see where you have been in
your year.

☐ ME0072
Make a ghost town

Take photographs of your local area to make it look like a ghost town.

Stick your images on these pages.

Look north

Go to the nearest viewing point. Take a photo facing north, south, east and west. List what is different in each image below.

Stick your photos here.

Memorise a place

Using only your memory and a pencil,
draw a map of somewhere. Now explore
that place using only your map. What
did you include and exclude, enlarge and
shrink?

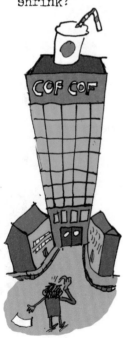

Make your area better

Set up a stall in your local market
to collect positive messages about your
local area. Invite some local journalists
to visit your stall and persuade them to
publish your findings.

Stick the newspaper report here.

Squeeze in

Fit as many people as you can into

a ....

How many people can you fit inside a:

1)

2)

3)

□ME0077
Play hide in shop

Go to a shopping centre and play hide-and-seek.

Which are the best three shops to hide in?

Visit a place of worship

...for 5 different religions.

What's similar?

What's different?

BE FRIENDLY: Call up, book an appointment and ask for a short tour!

See a place differently

Sit outdoors in a place you know well with a friend. Privately both spend a few minutes drawing a picture of the same view.

Do you both see the same things?

Go on a random adventure

Go on a journey into the unknown. Using only a coin for direction, turn left every time you flip a head and right when you toss a tail. What's the furthest you can get with 20 spins?

Where do you end up?

Look up

Stand in a high street and look up.
What's the largest number of people that
you can get looking up at any one time?

Place a soundtrack

Go somewhere with your music player.
Which tracks best fit this place?

Play your soundtrack out loud. What do
people think of your selection?

WARNING!

Remember to get permission.

Broadcast to the world

Make a documentary.
Post it on the Internet.

Record some of the comments people post
online below. For tips on staying safe
online visit: www.thinkuknow.co.uk

□ ME0084

Conduct an economic experiment

They say 'time is money'. Superglue a coin to the ground and record how long different people are willing to invest in trying to pick it up.

WARNING!

Remember to get permission before gluing your coin.

Use your flower power

Find some rough land and
turn it into a garden
of food and flowers in a
design of your choice.

Use this space to plan your new garden.

WARNING!

Always get permission from the land
owner before attempting this mission.

Play pavement games

Game 01: No slab twice - find a wide stretch of path with lots of paving slabs. Get from one side to the other as many times as you can without touching the same slab twice.

Game 02: Crack slabbing - get from A to B by only stepping on cracked slabs.

Game 03: Slabmines - secretly mark out 'landmines' on a stretch of path. Ask a friend to get from one side to the other without stepping on a 'landmine'.

Go on the wetter run

Do you get wetter if you run or walk
in the rain?

☐ **ME0088**

Record a place

...that is...

Quiet:

Happy:

Beautiful:

Friendly:

Content:

Small:

Round:

Write and perform a short play using the sounds you have recorded.

Buy, buy, buy

How many adverts do you see in one day?

If you did what they all asked how much would you end up spending?

If you earned.............. per hour, how many hours would you have to work to afford it all?

Hide a ....

Buy a simple old
jigsaw from a
charity shop, put it
together and draw
a map on its back
that leads someone
to something or
somewhere special.

Post or plant the pieces so that the
person finds them over a long period of
time. Make sure you're around when they
find the final piece of the jigsaw and
work it all out!

☐ME0091

Photograph something invisible

Make a list of things that are invisible
to the human eye. Using a camera,
attempt to capture all the things on
your list. Show your images to someone.
Can they guess the invisible things that
you have photographed.

Ask them to draw something invisible here.

Test your teachers

How many teachers know your name?
Award certificates to congratulate those
that get it right.

Save a place

Something being demolished in your
neighbourhood?

Photograph it and keep it alive forever.

Stick your photograph here.

Cross a wood

Travel from one side of a wood to the other using only roots and branches. Every time you touch the ground lose a point.

WARNING!

Falling from trees can be very, very painful. Remember, do not climb: too high (the higher you go, the harder the fall), or when it's wet (you are more likely to slip) and avoid dead trees (they break easily).

Sit smart

Get together with some friends and sit silently and neatly in a public place.

Create a monument

Explore the monuments in your local area. What local histories do they reveal? Use this page to design and then make your own monument. How do people react to it?

Draw a local fantasy map

Create a map of your local area below,
but make it even
more fantastic. Keep
some features the
same, but add, move
and change others.
Ask your local
library to list and
display your map.

☐ ME0098

Set up a legal graffiti wall

Photograph the wall each day to see how it changes. Use a computer to turn your photos into a stop-motion video about the wall.

Create a well-placed mash-up

Create a beat, song and perhaps a tune about a place. Get permission and perform it there.

Don't scare the birds

Walk through a crowd of birds without getting a single one of them into a flap. If you do, start again.

Create a treasure map

Bury some treasure and draw a map so someone can find it. Secretly post the map through their door.

Get into the news

...by completing one of the
missions in this book.

Stick the news article here.

Discover more missions at
www.missionexplore.co.uk

My Missions:

My Missions:

175

Notes:

Notes:

Basic training:
First aid

Basic training: First aid

What to do when you get hurt...

Injured in the name of exploration? Here's some useful advice to follow. In all cases, tell someone you trust what happened and get checked out. Even the bravest and most famous explorers need a bit of looking after, especially if it involves some hot chocolate and cake.

Over the next few pages you can find out some basic things to help tackle:

1. Bleeding
2. Broken bones
3. Burns
4. Poisoning
5. Suffocating and choking
6. Insect bites and stings
7. Drowning

1. Bleeding

Blood rushing out of your body?
Remember two simple steps:

- Put pressure on the cut.

- Raise the cut above your heart.
  If it's your leg that's bleeding lie on
  your back and lift your legs.

If it's your head that's hurt put
pressure on the cut to stop the bleeding
and make sure that you get checked out
by the doctor. When asked how you did
it remember to tell the doctor all about
your amazing, death-defying mission!

2. Broken bones

Arm in howling pain, and can't
remember any fancy bandage work?

Don't panic!
Don't move the affected arm or leg.
Find a comfortable position to hold it
and then get help. It's a trip to the
hospital for you.

Make a note of where you are and phone
your emergency contact. The more you
move the more a broken bone will hurt -
so try to be like a stone.

Broken bones and bleeding?
Follow advice from 1 and 2.

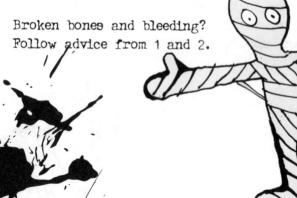

3. Burns

Had an encounter with
something too hot?
You need to get the affected
area into cold water fast.
If you are close to home
that's no problem, just run
your burnt bit under the
cold tap for 10 minutes.

Nowhere near home?
Try to find a stream or use
taps in a public building.
Afterward, check the burnt
bit and keep it clean
but don't put any fuzzy
bandages on it if you value
your lovely skin!

Make sure that you show
your burn to someone who
knows about burns, you may
well need to go to hospital.

4. Poisoned

Eaten or drunk something and feeling dodgy?

It's a trip to the doctor for you. Don't forget to grab the container of what you swallowed.

5. Suffocating & choking

Swallowed something stubborn?
Follow these steps.

1. Try to cough the pesky piece up, and if that does not work...

2. Get somebody to slap you on the back while you bend forwards. Five hard slaps between the shoulder blades should do the trick, but if that doesn't work...

3. Get help
Don't go running in doing the Heimlich manoeuvre you've seen in that cool movie - this one's only for the pros so get yourself trained first!

6. Stings or bites

You don't have to be in the jungle to have your arm bitten off by a ravenous beast. Even the smallest critter can leave you feeling quite sore.

First, check if any of your mates are allergic to any bites. If they are, they will have an epi-pen. Make sure you know what to do!

Otherwise, your bitten bit may swell up, so keep it elevated above your head.

If you have been bitten by something poisonous call for help and get to a doctor as soon as you can.

7. Drowning

Water can be one of the most deadly of
substances. If you can't swim don't go
in. It's that simple! Water can be one of
the most deadly of substances. Even if
you are a good swimmer, cold water and
water currents can make it a lot more
difficult. If you can't swim don't get
too close. Many people get into trouble
because they trip or fall near the edge
and end up falling in.

Just been rescued from drowning?
Get to the hospital and let them check
you out as soon as you can.

Dangerous people

Most people you will encounter on your missions will be quite safe. Most people in the world are. But, just to be certain, don't get into anyone's car that you don't know. Ever. Most importantly, don't agree to go into anyone's house without the permission of the people who look after you.

Safe people

Most adults are safe to ask for help
from. If you get hurt or run into
trouble the vast majority of adults
will be able to help you but the best
people to ask are those in the emergency
services. If they're not around ask a
group of adults in a public place.

Dangerous places

There are lots of signs that warn
you of hazards. Follow their advice.
High, slippery, electric, explosive,
sharp, mean and very hot places
should be avoided, without special
training.

Safe places

Whenever you feel you need help public
buildings are always a great place to
head for. Hospitals, police stations,
schools and libraries tend to be full of
people who will be able to help you
in your moment of need.

Advanced training organisations in the UK

For more, visit www.missionexplore.co.uk

British Mountaineering Council
www.thebmc.co.uk

British Canoe Union
www.bcu.org.uk

Duke of Edinburgh's Award
www.dofe.org

Earthwatch
www.earthwatch.org

Field Studies Council
www.field-studies-council.org

Girl Guides
www.girlguiding.org.uk

Red Cross
www.redcross.org.uk

Royal Geographical Society
www.rgs.org

Royal Society for the
Protection of Birds
www.rspb.org.uk

Royal Yachting Association
www.rya.org.uk

Scouts
www.scouts.org.uk

Sports Leaders
www.bst.org.uk

St John Ambulance
www.sja.org.uk/sja

Wildlife Trusts
www.wildlifetrusts.org

Woodcraft Folk
www.woodcraft.org.uk

Youth Hostel Association
www.yha.org.uk

The Geography Collective

We're a bunch of Guerrilla Geographers. We've written this book because we think it's really fun and important to get exploring and questioning the world. We do hope that you like it and get it really dirty and full of your mission reports. We'd love to hear from you to discover how your missions have gone.

MISSION:EXPLORE creators are Alan, Daniel, David, Duncan, James, Kye, Menah, Simon, Tom and Tony. A band of geography explorers, doctors, artists, teachers, activists, adventurers and other things.

Our wonderful drawings and ink splats are by Tom, also known as Inky Mess. At Can of Worms Kids Press, Emily has done our design, Helen has brought it all together and Tobias has put trust in us.

This edition of MISSION:EXPLORE has been directed by Daniel.

To find out more about us, file or
report or to get in touch visit
www.geographycollective.co.uk.

Visit www.missionexplore.co.uk to:
- submit mission reports
- discover bonus missions
- get missions on your mobile
- explore mapped missions

If you are old enough, follow
MISSION:EXPLORE on Twitter at:
@missionexplore

Thanks go out to: BZD-j, Sebastian, Sally,
Ella, Sam, Hilary, David, Mam, Mary,
Anthony, Eliz, David, Sarah, Curly,
Shizzer, Nicola and John at CSEC, Helen,
Emily, Dan, Tobias, Mythical Pete, Toby,
Dennis, Elaine, Jon, Jenny, Mark and
The Workshop.

About Can of Worms

As the name suggests Can of Worms is a wriggling writing collective of book publishers. We have stories about ordinary people doing extraordinary things: climbing mountains, finding cannibals, cycling around the world and other amazing adventures, all published by Eye Books.

We also do wonderful fun comic versions of Shakespeare's plays illustrated by more fantastic people and we even have stories about a bionic cat called Boing-Boing, published by Can of Worms Kids Press.

You can find out more and get special offers on our books at:
www.canofwormsenterprises.co.uk

Free e-book

To get a completely free online e-book copy of Mission:Exlore, drop us a line at explore@canofwormsenterprises.co.uk

Being friendly to our environment

We take being friendly to our planet
seriously. No animals were hurt in the
making of this book and we have been
very careful with how we use trees.
We have only used paper made from
sustainable sources.

And while we love exploring the world,
we have printed the book locally in
the UK so not to pour lots of carbon
into the atmosphere on planes, boats and
trucks.

A few more words on recycling

All the words in Mission:Explore have
been recycled. You will have seen most of
them elsewhere but if not you can find
them in a dictionary. Please feel free
to send us any words you might wish at
explore@canofwormsenterprises.co.uk

Want more?

You could check out our other book, the Journey Journal....

Going somewhere new is a massive opportunity to discover & make sense of cultures, environments, issues and alternative ideas. Journey Journal is a special passport-sized book that encourages you to (re)think the places you visit.

Or, how about a MISSION:EXPLORE club?

Running a MISSION:EXPLORE club is easy. Just follow these steps:

1. Get some people together. Ideally some you know and some you don't.
2. Go out and complete MISSION:EXPLORE missions. Create some of your own.
3. Share how you've got on.